Japan

An Insider's Guide for the Savvy Traveler

Dave Dunne

Table of Contents

Preface

Japan. A country full of history, mystery, experiences, and culture unlike any other. It's been said that one could spend many lifetimes exploring Japan and just barely scratch the surface. Unfortunately, we don't have that much time.

This concise, to-the-point guide full of insider information, tips and tricks will give you a good starting point to plan from and minimize the learning curve during your journey through what can be a very overwhelming destination.

The 40 Minute Travel Guide ™ series was inspired by my desire to share my insights and lessons learned during my many travels and time spent living in various countries around Asia. This is not a thorough guide book, nor is it a complete history lesson. You will not find detailed maps and tours in this book. What you **WILL** find is information you would *ONLY* know if you'd lived here or spent lots of time here, which will make your trip much smoother than it would be, had you *NOT* read this book.

Japan: An Insider's Guide for the Savvy Traveler is designed to be read in around **40 Minutes,** give or take, depending on your reading speed. The reason for this is simple: That's all the time you need to effectively absorb the required "to-the-point" and "must-know" information. This includes:

- Brief history and culture lesson;

- Must-know customs, laws, acceptable behavior AND a list of DOs and DON'Ts;

- Tips and tricks for getting around, keeping out of trouble and staying safe;

- Recommended preparations, destinations, how to get there, how to best enjoy them;

- Birdseye view of the best food and entertainment in each area; and

- General pointers that one would ONLY know from learning the hard way.

I would highly recommend also downloading the eBook version of this book, for the many helpful links to external sites, articles and maps that you'll need to utilize. Also, visit 40minutetravelguru.com for some of the same links and information. Safe travels!

Introduction

"I often compare the experience of going to Japan for the first time to what Eric Clapton and Pete Townsend must have gone through the first time Jimi Hendrix came to town. You hear about it, you go see it, a whole window opens up into a whole new thing, and you think: what does this mean, what do I have left to say, what do I do now."

-Anthony Bourdain

If you've bought this book, odds are that you're either planning a trip to Japan or are considering doing so. Having lived in Japan for upwards of 6 years, I can easily say that it is one of my favorite places on the earth, if not my favorite. Between the welcoming and warm attitude of the people, the natural beauty from the beaches to the mountains, and the seemingly endless and out-of-this-world nightlife, I believe that all people should visit Japan at least once in their lives. Those of us who have spent time living there are lucky indeed.

It is for this reason, and my intimate familiarity, that I have chosen to make Japan the first country in this series of books. One could spend lifetimes in Japan and only scratch the surface. I was fortunate enough to have lived there long enough, and develop the kinds of friendships, which allowed me to get much deeper than a traveler or short time expat would have the opportunity to.

In general, Japan is an incredibly safe and easy place to visit, and to live. The crime rate is EXTREMELY low (I didn't lock my car doors, and if I forgot to lock my house at night I would not lose any sleep), the people are the nicest on the planet, and transportation around the country is simple (with the exception of the train system in Tokyo, which we will discuss later). That said, not everyone speaks the best English (but most have a very basic grasp), and it can be a very expensive place, especially compared to other destinations around Asia. For these reasons, the focus of this book will be on:

- How to enjoy your time in the smoothest and most problem-free way possible

- Transportation and Accommodations

- Where to go and what to do

- Everyday must-knows, tips, and tricks

And less on:

- Staying safe and avoiding trouble

To truly understand Japan, and the Japanese people, we must first look at a brief history of Japan leading up to the modern day, and how this history has shaped the country and its relationships with the outside world and with tourism.

Transformation into a Tourism Destination

From Samurai to Salaryman

Prior to the year 1868, Japan was a hermit-like nation. It had successfully repelled foreign invaders and influence for centuries, a time defined by warring feudal lords and the samurai "bushido" code of honor. Fearing that they would be left behind by advancing technologies from the West, the Emperor agreed to open Japan up to external trade in 1868. This change in status quo known as the "Meiji Restoration" (named for Emperor Meiji) would inevitably lead to the rise of the Japanese Empire, and a shift in Japan from a feudal society to a more Westernized society as it pertains to government, industry, military and foreign relations. This is key to understanding Japan, as the old traditions and "code of honor" from the pre-Meiji period was not lost.

Of course, fast forward to World War 2. After the war, the US occupied the country, changed the form of government and influenced Japan in a way that had been yet unseen. Japan absorbed a taste for American foods, culture, entertainment and became intertwined with the US in both governments, military, and industry. This relationship has morphed in the decades since into an alliance and business relationship that is strong today.

Through this, Japan still retains its customs and culture from previous history. In fact, Japan is possibly the only place in the world that has so drastically evolved into a Westernized nation and retained so much of its cultural identity. Modern Japan is one that contains deep and visible roots in its feudal history and traditions, as well as the influences of the West. A great example of this would be witnessing a group of young Japanese girls dressed in summertime "yukata" (similar to a kimono), after leaving a traditional Japanese summer event, eating at McDonald's, listening to Taylor Swift and using words like "Cool" and "Bye Bye."

Though Western influence is strong, Japanese people are incredibly proud of their long-standing values and traditions which are alive, visible and ingrained into modern Japan. Japanese people treat tourists with the utmost respect and expect visitors to also respect their culture and traditions. A little bit of respect goes a very long way in Japan.

Japanese Culture

This first thing you'll notice about the people in Japan is how polite they are. This politeness comes from a deep-rooted concept of respect and putting the group first before the individual and transcends everything about daily life in the country. Respect for others is why people form a line when waiting or step outside to talk on the phone. The idea of being bothersome to others is highly offensive to Japanese people. This concept is the reason why punctuality is important, acts of kindness and courteousness go so far and why as a foreigner, observing and mimicking these positive behaviors will both give you a new perspective on respect and earn you respect from your hosts.

A few more key aspects of Japanese culture and behavior one should know:

- Japan is still a very male-dominated society; however, this is slowly changing. Japan could be compared to the 1960s in this regard.

- Saving face, as everywhere in Asia, is an important concept to practice. This entails saving one from embarrassment in front of others. Don't ever embarrass someone or make them look bad, doing so can be deadly, really. With that in mind, "Yes" does not always mean "Yes" in Japan. The word "Hai" or a head nod may be a way for someone to simply avoid saying "No" to allow for you to save face. Doublecheck by asking "ii desuka?" *(ee-des-ka)* (See Translation section below) to confirm the situation.

- In Japan, the old saying "The nail that sticks out the most gets the hammer" is entirely accurate. Japanese people are EXTREMELY law-abiding and obedient. Rules are never broken and socially frowned upon behavior is almost never acted upon. This concept tends to create a pack mentality both socially and in the workplace: Individual innovation or bravery is very rare. (Example: I have seen many altercations in Japan that would have been interfered with by bystanders in other countries, but here, either for the desire to not bother anyone or fear of sticking out, nobody got involved except myself or another foreigner).

- Japanese people tend to be intrigued by foreigners and can come off at first as a bit xenophobic or mildly obsessed, depending on which view they have. Keep in mind that some of this behavior is due to the country being closed off to foreigners before the mid-1800s, and the widespread desire to maintain a homogenous society to keep their culture intact. The most exposure some people in Japan, rural areas mostly, have had to foreigners is in movies. That's why the kids are staring at you.

Japanese Views of Foreigners and Stereotypes

In addition to the rich culture and traditions still strong in Japan today, the mindset and stereotypes towards foreigners present during the Shogunate days are still somewhat ingrained into the psyche of many Japanese people. Not harmful in the slightest, think of this mindset as not in the forefront of a Japanese person's thoughts but embedded in the background. Some of the opinions and mindsets you are likely to encounter are:

- *Foreigners are outsiders*: Gaijin or gaijin-san, a term you will hear often, directly translates to "outsider", and yes, they are talking about you. Above all other aspects of the Japanese views on foreigners discussed here, this is the most important. This mindset has its roots in the pre-Meiji restoration era when Japan was completely insulated from the world, and foreigners were not to be trusted or allowed to enter the country. This term is not entirely negative all the time, as it is commonly used when a Japanese person may express that a foreigner does not speak Japanese or doesn't understand a particular cultural aspect when speaking to other Japanese people.

*When traveling in other countries, it is common to hear Japanese people refer to the local people in that country as "Gaijin" which is simply comical and should help this idea sink in.

- *Japanese Pride*: Many Asian countries have been at odds with one another for a very long time, and specifically, some sentiments remain from World War 2 in this regard. An additional basis for this lies in the above "Gaijin" ideas, and also from a nationalistic pride that the Japanese have ingrained in them from turning their economy into the economic powerhouse that it is today from the post-war era. Put more simply, they may have a slight ego when it comes to Asian and international relations. At the end of the day, Japanese people tend to be incredibly proud of their Japan, and there is nothing wrong with that. It is truly a magical place.

- *Foreign Stereotypes:* In general, Japanese people are just as susceptible to belief in stereotypes as anyone. This combined with their overall obedient nature gives them little reason to question, so they mostly believe and embrace them all. This can, at times, play to your advantage

11

of course. From England? You can easily be a Football player if you want. From Texas? Expect people think you're a cowboy. Some examples:

1. *American Cool:* The two countries have a longstanding relationship which has resulted in the widespread popularity of American entertainment. This includes mostly Hollywood movies, rap, pop music, and sports. Baseball is by far the most popular sport in Japan. Burgers and fries are a treat. If you're from New York or LA, expect to that to impress people for no reason at all.

2. *European Class:* In Japan, owning any products imported from Europe (particularly France) are, in Japanese minds, a status symbol. Of course, this is not restricted to Japan; however, in Japan, it's another level. Anything to do with Europe is considered classy.

There are, of course, some negatives to the stereotyping that comes with being a foreigner in Japan. Though they can become frustrating if you live in Japan, you should not be too impacted during your travels, unless you may be denied entry to some nightlife establishments which may be reserved for Japanese patrons only. As an example, prepare for the below to happen:

- You may be assumed to know everything about and everyone in your country, to include all relevant or irrelevant music, movies, and other pop culture. People will ask you things like "Do you know Johnny Depp?" or something similar. Let them down gently.

- People may act/ be scared of you. This usually is resultant from not actually knowing any foreigners or a long history of stories of foreigners doing some fairly bad things. Acting loud and brazenly will not help this. This is more common in rural areas. Smile and nod.

- Be prepared to not be allowed into some establishments. I have found that in most cases it's because the staff doesn't speak English or the activities in the place are reserved for locals.

- School children and kids will stare at you, or even ask to take selfies. Some simply don't know what you are, and others may speak English to you or think you're an English teacher. It's cute really.

- Everyone and I mean everyone, will assume you don't speak any Japanese. If you have an even remotely Asian looking person in your group (to include dark tanned Caucasians), they will by default become the communicator in the eyes of the locals. Even if you speak fluent Japanese and they don't speak any. This is a very odd phenomenon.

- If you're below 30 and a man with short hair, prepare for everyone to think you're a US servicemember. In some places, they'll also suspect that you're drunk and looking for women, no matter what time of day.

Modern Tourism

With 21 World Heritage Sites and some of the best food and nightlife in the world, Japan has much to offer in the way of tourism and is increasing in popularity among regional Asian travelers as a tourism destination. As English-speaking countries go, the US comes in 5th with Australia coming in 7th for numbers of tourists each year. As Japan is making efforts to increase tourism, nearby countries seem to be increasing their travels. 50% of tourists to Japan come from China and South Korea. This will be evident at any international airport and is the case all over Asia. I would highly recommend avoiding these crowds at all costs, though this is becoming increasingly difficult at the most famous of sites. Thankfully, these groups come in tours and typically have their own buses, travel arrangements and don't clog up the train systems.

Geographic Overview

Mainland Japan consists of 4 main islands:

• **Hokkaido:** The Northernmost island and accessible via air or rail, very comparable to Alaska in terms of weather, industry, and tourism. The major city is Sapporo, and the island is most famous for its seafood (again, think Alaska), wildlife, mountains, snow and winter sports.

- **Honshu:** The largest and most populated island containing most of the major cities. The interior is mountainous and most of the population resides in the cities and towns along the coast. The entire island is serviced by the Shinkansen "Bullet Train" lines.

- **Shikoku:** Smallest of the 4 islands and located below Osaka and to the Southeast of the lower part of Honshu. Also containing a mountainous interior, only accessible via expressway, ferry, and air. Matsuyama is the major city in Shikoku.

- **Kyushu:** The Southern island most famous for its many Onsens and volcanic activity. The major cities in Kyushu are Fukuoka, Kitakyushu, and Kumamoto. Nagasaki is also located in Kyushu.

The **Ryukyu Islands** in the South (closer to Taiwan than Japan) consist of many small tropical islands, the main of which is Okinawa. The Ryukyus are a popular destination within Japan and internationally.

Preparations

Toiletries

Any toiletries you may need can be found in Japan. Even toothbrushes and toothpaste are provided in every hotel room. What you may need, you can certainly find at any convenience store or "conbini" (*cone-beanie*) located literally on almost every block in every city. These are discussed further later in the book.

Healthcare

Though healthcare is considerably cheaper in Japan than most places, you should get set up and make sure you're covered by your insurance carrier. If you should find yourself in need of healthcare, your first priority should be to find sufficient translation. Though some hospitals do have translators on staff, most do not, and you will have an incredibly difficult time trying this on your own. If an emergency, try and find the largest hospital around, as this will increase your chances they have a translator. Translation is discussed later in this section. For a clinic or pharmacy, look for the **GREEN** cross, not the red one.

If you do need to visit a hospital, expect some surprises along the way. They may ask you to do things that seem unnecessary, not speak to other doctors when they should, and generally confuse you. Just be polite, patient and remain calm and the situation should eventually get resolved. They're pretty smart people.

Medications and Vaccines

As Japan is a very clean and non-tropical country (mainland), no special vaccinations should be required unless you plan to spend lots of time in the mountains or the tropical islands of the southern Ryukyu Islands. It would be smart to bring enough of any medications you may need; however, should you need to obtain a prescription, a visit to a Japanese hospital may be needed. You should note that many prescription AND over-the-counter medicines are not legal in Japan, with or without an outside prescription. Check the Japanese Embassy site prior to traveling with any medications, as if you're caught it will get you in some trouble. Drugs are one thing they don't mess with in Japan.

Translation

Though English is a popular language, and many people have a basic grasp of key words like "Hello" and "Please," you may find yourself in need of translation or interpreter services while in Japan. I recommend Craigslist or any plethora of internet translation sites which have translators in major cities. If you strike out, check with a local English school (there are plenty) and they may be able to set you up. Expect to pay upwards of 50USD/ hour for professional services, which is worth every dollar for a medical situation. If you are seeking an interpreter for a tour or other activity, I recommend TripAdvisor as a good resource.

Translation Apps

There is currently a multitude of apps available to aid in translation, and I have found none of the mobile phone apps to work well, though Google translate can get you by with the occasional strange look. I would recommend one that has high reviews and is capable of working offline. If you use Google translator, use simple sentences when using these apps as the meaning can easily become very construed when translated into Japanese. Keep it simple.

Do: "Where is the train station?"

Do not: "Do you know where the nearest train station is."

Alternatively, I can personally vouch (and I wish I had this years ago) for a few translation devices for quick operation, long battery life, offline mode (this is a Godsend) **AND** human-like translation. As someone who has worked with numerous interpreters, the human aspect of translation is something most apps fail at. Visit the resources page at 40minutetravelguru.com for specific products.

Emergency Numbers

Emergency numbers in Japan are the same everywhere. The only difference will be how quickly they can get an English speaker on the line. Obviously, you will need to have cellular service for this work (discussed later):

Fire and Ambulance: 119

Police: 110

Key Phrases

For a list of must-know phrases in Japanese, I recommend downloading a well-rated app to study on the plane ride over. Japanese Slanguage is a very good one. Some key phrases you do need to know:

- **Sumimasen** *(soo-mee-ma-sin):* Pardon me

- **Arigato** *(ah-ree-gato)*: Thank you

- **Daijobu** *(die-joe-boo):* Fine, okay

- **Desu/ desuka** *(des/des-ka)*: A state of being or is. Adding the "ka" turns into a question. Saying "Bob desu" means "I am Bob."

- **Daijobu desuka?**: Are you okay?

- **Ii desuka?** *(ee-des-ka)***:** Is it okay?

- **Hai** *(high):* An acknowledgment

- **Gomen-nasai** *(ego-min-na-sigh)*: Sorry, with admittance for wrongdoing

19

- **Eigo no menyu arimasuka?** *(ego-min-oo-ari-mas-ka):* Do you have an English menu (Eigo = English)

- **Onegaishimasu** *(Oh-ne-guy-she-mas)*: Please

- **Toire** *(Toy-lay)*: The toilet

- **Doko**: Where? *(ex. "Toire doko desuka?" = Where is the toilet?)*

Transportation

Public transportation in Japan is a system which every country in the world should study and model their systems after. Besides the cleanliness and safety, you can literally set your watch by the train schedules: They are almost NEVER late, and the Japanese take this very seriously. Being such a punctual people, there are incredibly harsh punishments for individuals who cause trains or buses to be delayed (don't touch that emergency stop). Efficient travel in Japan will include use of all of the available transportation methods.

The **Shinkansen** (bullet train) is a popular and fun method to see the country and get from city to city once you've landed. As the main cities in Japan are generally positioned on the coast, the Shinkansen runs North to South, hitting most major cities from the top to the bottom. Note that if you're going very far, and not stopping in between cities, it is probably more economical to fly if you have not bought a **JR Rail Pass**. JR Railways (which owns most railways in Japan) offers a 7- or 14-day JR Pass at a

STEEP discount to tourists who reserve passes in advance (Note: These must be mailed to your home country address and can take a few weeks, so order way in advance). If you're doing much traveling, this is a must and will save you hundreds of dollars. Additionally, the Green Car (think 1st class train ticket) can be gotten for not much more than the standard non-reserved seats where you run the risk of having to stand during high travel times. This is highly worth it for access to the entire country's high-speed rail system.

For travel within cities and rural areas, the **Local Trains** are going to be your method. I would highly recommend downloading the free application **HyperDia** for mapping out your trips on the local trains, especially for travel within the cities. Japan's city train systems can become quite complicated without the use of this app. Even natives frequently become lost, and I personally do not know how people got around Tokyo prior to this app. The local trains are much more economical than the taxis and have stops scattered all over most sizeable cities. The best way to get around is to utilize the local trains until you are forced to use a taxi to complete your journey. The Tokyo train system is a topic of its own and is discussed in detail in the Tokyo section of this book.

Taxis are expensive in Japan and should only be used when they must, or out of convenience if money is no object. To put this into perspective: A 1-hour taxi may cost the Yen equivalent of 100 USD, while the same distance covered in a local train will cost around 10 USD in the same amount of time. You can usually expect a very polite older man with white gloves as a driver, and expect to have to explain your destination, or show him a map and/ or name and address written and easy to read with bad eyesight. Hailing a taxi in Japan is the same as any other country. Outside of train stations, there will be a pickup point for taxis, and the line will be evident for this when you see it. Don't cut this line.

Taxi Tip: A taxi with a RED light in the front indicates that it is available. A GREEN light indicates that it has an occupant. GREEN does not mean GO, except that this taxi will go right on past you.

Uber has recently broken into the Japanese market, to the scorn of many a taxi company owning politician. This is (as of this writing) Tokyo only, but expect this to spread to other major cities.

Buses are an option for cheap travel within and between cities; however, can be very confusing as not many foreigners choose this option, and bus schedules and routes are rarely in English. Within Cities, buses typically start/ end their route at main train stations. Upon entering the bus, a small machine near the door will eject a ticket, which you should take and keep. During the trip, a monitor at the front of the bus will tally the cost as the bus makes progress through the route. Upon arrival at your destination, which will be announced by the driver (not in English), you will need to depart the forward door (near the driver) and deposit the bus fare IN COINS into the machine. If you don't have change, the machine will provide you change for small Yen notes (1-5,000 yen) for which you will need to then deposit the correct change in the machine. Do not carry 10,000 yen notes and expect change. Bottom line: Try to avoid within the city.

Buses between cities usually depart and arrive at the main train stations in each City/ Town, and the station staff will happily assist you, or, to research or book a bus trip in advance, I recommend japanbuslines.com. Buses are also a convenient means to and from main train hubs and airports.

IC Cards are the most convenient way to pay for public transportation. These are rechargeable cards that can be purchased at the same point-of-sale machines as a ticket and can be used for local trains, Shinkansen, buses, (some) taxis and even some vending machines and convenience stores. These are simply scanned across a reader at the entry and exit point of the train station or point of sale. Look for the sign at the ticket reader indicating which cards are accepted. Note that there are 3 main cards, for use in different regions and with different transportation companies.

The main cards I would recommend you buy, depending on your locations are **Suica** and **Pasmo** for the Tokyo area, **Icoca** for the Chugoko/ Osaka/ Kyoto area and **Sugoku** for the Kyushu region (South). I recommend routinely checking your balance and topping off at the ticket machines. If you happen to need to top off while inside of the system and are denied exit due to insufficient funds on the card, look for the yellow "Fare Adjustment" machine. Travel Payment can, of course, be made at each station, bus or taxi. This is a very inconvenient way to get around. I highly recommend purchasing an IC Card, which can make getting around much more efficient and less of a headache.

There are also a number of domestic **Airlines** flying within Japan, some at very low rates. These include:

- Japan Airlines and All Nippon Airlines (ANA): Both carriers offer discounted tickets, for travel within Japan, for foreign tourists. To book this, you must book in advance, on the US site (linked above) from outside of Japan, or from a VPN within Japan, and provide your international airline ticket number at the time of booking.

- Peach Airlines: Peach is a discount domestic carrier that operates between most sizeable cities in Japan. A good option if time is of the essence or the Shinkansen is not an option (We're talking about you Okinawa). Peach offers regular deals on travel internationally from Japan also.

- Other carriers include Skymark, Jet Star, Vanilla Air, and Air Asia.

Some advice with regard to the discount airlines: Be mindful of your luggage allotment. A discount rate can quickly turn into a standard rate or worse if proper attention is not paid to maximum baggage weight.

Technology

In addition to downloading the **HyperDia** app above, (and in order to use it upon arrival) you should ensure that you will have cellular or Wi-Fi service once you hit the ground. I cannot stress this enough. For this, there are a few options:

- Pick up a SIM at any cellular service stand either at the airport or at any **Bic Camera** store located throughout most cities. The stores found in the airports can be very overpriced, so do some shopping around. I have found that the stores immediately near the exits are the most expensive, while stores located in upper floors in the Narita airport (which would not be normally visited by arriving passengers) can be half the price; HOWEVER, you will need to set up the SIM yourself. If you cannot do that, choose the more expensive option and do not leave until they show you that it is working. Packages are offered based on maximum data usage for a set amount of time. Choose wisely. Maps and other apps you will need to be running frequently use a lot of data.

- Preorder a data-only SIM card for your phone for pickup upon arrival at the airport or hotel. You can arrange this for pickup at any of the large airports in advance. More information can be found at Tokyocheapo.com.

- Rent a pocket Wi-Fi upon arrival. Japan Wi-Fi Buddy is a good service for this but must be booked in advance for delivery to your hotel or airport. This can be dropped in the mail when your trip is complete.

- Bring a means to charge your phone on the go. Exploring in Japan requires heavy phone application use which will quickly drain your battery. Do not be caught in transit without a means to find your way.

Many establishments have free Wi-Fi, and you should be able to connect to the free Airport Wi-Fi immediately upon exiting your plane. Connect to Wi-Fi when you can to save your cellular data usage, as the SIM card packages usually have a maximum limit on them.

Driving in Japan

Something I don't advise for a tourist, but International Drivers Permits must be obtained prior to arrival in Japan if you plan on renting a car at any point in time. Again, I HIGHLY advise against it. I only recommend this as an option if you plan on going off the beaten path, visiting an area that does not have adequate public transportation or otherwise. Due to further complications with translation and toll roads that you will NOT be prepared to deal with, I highly advise planning your trip to NOT include any substantial time with a rental car. BUT IF YOU MUST, make sure this is clearly booked in advance and you arrive at the rental agency with paperwork in hand. If you do decide to rent a car, you should thoroughly familiarize yourself with driving in Japan, the rules are quite different and the consequences of making a mistake can be quite harsh. Obviously, check the requirements in your home country and ensure to have your own GPS capability along with you.

Accommodations

Japan has many different accommodation types that you should be aware of. Each type has its own experience and cost associated with it, and this should help you decide which type you would like to pursue. Few things on hotels in Japan:

- Choose a hotel with breakfast. It is SOOOO worth it.
- Hotel rooms can be considered somewhat cramped in Japan. Keep this in mind if you are traveling with lots of luggage or a travel partner (don't ever, ever, ever get a single). Look at the photos before booking.
- Many hotels have more than one location in each city. Take note of this when you begin to communicate to drivers, etc. what your destination is. Have it mapped out or written down to show the driver or a helpful citizen. (Ex. Tokyo must have at least 80 APA Hotels)
- Japanese hotels provide all the toiletries that you need and even have in-call massage services and food delivery menus in the room.

Throughout the book, I will provide my recommendations where it makes sense, based on budget and location, for each area discussed. Of note, hotel prices in Japan are highly sensitive to market conditions, meaning, prices can drastically change based on fluctuations in occupancy rates and how far in advance a booking is made. It is not uncommon to see a hotel price increase 200% in a matter of days leading up to the weekend, especially in Tokyo. For hotel bookings in Japan, I recommend Agoda, as they seem to have many Japanese hotels on the site not found on other travel sites, and provide a confirmation with the address in Japanese you may save as an image on your phone. Handy for asking directions with no phone service. Below is my brief explanation of the types of accommodation you can find in Japan:

- **Luxury Hotels**: 200-1,000 USD/ night. Hilton, Sheraton, Hyatt, Westin, and others. All have locations in most cities.

- **Mid-range**: 100-200 USD/ night. APA Hotels, Rihga Royal, Mitsui Garden, Washington, Tokyu. These chains have locations in every city and I have found them all to be a good value. APA Hotels specifically has many locations, is always well priced, well maintained and kept looking new. Rihga Royal Hotels typically have a high-end restaurant and shopping offerings on premises that make it very convenient and a great value.

- **Budget/ Business Hotels**: 50-100 USD/ night. Flexstays, My Stay, Villa Fontaine, Dormy Inn, Toyoku, Sunroute. These hotels are typically single bed, cramped and a bit on the aged side, but well priced and with the same basic amenities as most other hotels.

- **Capsule Hotels**: 25-75 USD/ night. The capsule hotel is an accommodation type specific to Japan, a result of the limited space available and a plethora of people regularly needing a cheap place to rest. The sleeping quarters resemble an entire wall of small (roughly 4FT x 4FT x 7FT) but private capsules containing a mattress, lighting controls, alarm clock, outlets, small space to store a bag and sometimes even a TV. The capsules are stacked and laid side by side, on top of one another. You enter it from the front, separated by an operable divider located at the front opening. The living areas are segregated into male and female, each with its own common use bathing and toilet facilities.

  Capsule hotels are an experience indeed, mostly used by budget salarymen, tourists, those that have missed the last train for the night or simply didn't plan in advance and cannot afford the hotel room that shot up 200% in price. I recommend you stay in a capsule hotel one time. Some are actually quite enjoyable and can be quite convenient if you only need a place to catch a few hours of sleep.

- **24 Hour Internet Cafes and Karaoke Rooms**: Low budget. These options may come as a surprise to you and should only be considered as a last resort to get off of the street and catch a few hours' sleep in an emergency. Though not officially geared towards overnight stays, these facilities do provide either a bed or basic sofa(s) and can be paid for cheaply for a quick overnight stay or couple hours of sleep. Japanese people do this frequently (usually due to missing the last train).

For karaoke rooms, ask for "free time," which means that you pay for 3 hours, but the time is free after that until a certain time the following day (more on karaoke rooms later in the book). For internet cafes, these are more suitable for single travelers and make sure they have a futon or sofa prior to making payment.

- **Love Hotels** (*Rabuho*): 50-200 USD/ night. If you did not already know about love hotels, please allow me to explain. Love hotels are a very common type of short-stay hotel in Japan without nearly the stigma such a thing may have in your home country. Strictly for couples (you cannot go to a love hotel alone), love hotels offer a discreet stay in a room that is either decorated in high-end décor or "themed" (think robots, mirrors, schoolgirls, maids, UFO's, jungles, Hello Kitty and even Winnie the Pooh). Love hotels are frequented by everyone from young couples living with their parents (and no privacy) to secret lovers, club connections and prostitutes. Most love hotels offer a wide selection of room service, beverages and many contain lavish jacuzzies, shower rooms, and in-room karaoke. Love hotels can be priced for a "rest" (a few hours) or a "stay" (overnight). Discretion is the main theme at all love hotels, and interaction with staff is non-existent.

You cannot book a love hotel in advance. To stay, you enter the lobby, review a panel displaying the types of rooms available, and make your selection before proceeding to the room as prompted. To check out, you provide your payment to the automated payment machine located in the room, which accepts cash, and (sometimes) card. This occurs at the end of your stay. There is no set checkout time and you can stay as long as you want once checked in. Most love hotels are located in and around the nightlife areas of each city and can be recognized by their abnormal names (almost always beginning with the word Hotel) and wildly themed exterior décor and architecture. I do recommend staying in one at least once; however, in highly dense cities such as Tokyo, expect these to be very full on the weekends. Forget the taboo associated with short stay hotels in your home country, these can be quite high class and always fun.

- **Ryokan** (City Guesthouse): 50-200 USD/ night. Ryokans are a very traditional Japanese inn experience, with tatami flooring, futon bedding (think a roll-up mattress, not a couch type futon), tea rooms and usually a very traditional dinner and/ or breakfast. Ryokan can be found all over Japan, catering to tourists and locals alike. Ryokan can be either City Ryokan, having a somewhat similar function and amenities as a hostel, or Onsen Ryokan, located in Onsen, or natural hot spring towns. As an

31

experience in and of itself, Ryokan are the most enjoyable in Onsen towns.

- **Onsen Ryokan** (Hot Spring Guesthouse): 100-500 USD/ night. Japanese Onsen, or natural hot spring baths, are common across the country, usually in the countryside, as Japan is a hotbed of volcanic activity. There are many types of Onsen, public, private, gender-segregated and mixed gender. Onsen Ryokan are a traditional way to enjoy the natural hot springs. Some (more expensive) Ryokan provide a private outdoor hot spring bath for your room, while others have public baths, reservation only baths and on-site or numerous private baths scattered about the property. The natural hot spring waters contain different nutrients in different parts of the country and are known to be incredibly healthy and rejuvenating. These Ryokans include a traditional dinner, breakfast and in-room tea amenities. I highly recommend taking advantage of this during your stay. A truly "can't miss" experience.

- **Hostels:** 20-50 USD/ night. Hostels catering to foreign travelers can be found all over Japan. This can be a very low budget way to explore the country and meet fellow travelers, share ideas, etc. Many hostels in Japan offer private rooms in addition to the shared rooms most people are familiar with.

- **Airbnb:** 30-300 USD/ night. Airbnb rentals are legal and gaining popularity in Japan. The available pool of Airbnb's varies across the different cities and neighborhoods and can often present a cost-friendly alternative to hotels, especially when traveling as a group.

For a thorough guide on hotels in Tokyo specifically, visit my page on the topic at 40minutetravelguru.com.

Money

Despite being a highly advanced society responsible for some of the most incredible technological advancements of modern times, Japan is surprisingly still a majority cash country. With that said, please note these money tips:

- Do not expect to be able to use your credit card at every establishment, and do not plan to be able to withdraw money from most ATMs. Most foreign ATM, Debit and Credit card cash withdrawals are possible at only 711 (look for the famous Orange and Green sign) and Family Mart ATM's, as well as ATM's located at the Post Offices scattered around. 711 and Family Mart can literally be found every 200 yards or so in every city and are also present in most small towns in Japan.

- If you are changing money upon arrival, do so at the airport, as you will not see many other money exchanges once you leave.

- Do not expect to be able to receive change for a 10,000 yen note. Try to accumulate smaller bills for use in taxis and any automated payment machines.

- Keep a minimum amount of cash handy for safe keeping, as you never know when you will need it in an emergency.

- Keep your cash in good condition. It is considered extremely rude to hand someone a wad of crumpled up bills.

Movies

I recommend watching the following movies before you visit Japan, just to pair up the concepts you will see in this book with what you see in the movie for a better learning experience about the culture and your trip. The below are available on Amazon or many other places. Just watch anyway you can.

- Lost in Translation

- The Last Samurai

- Jiro Dreams of Sushi

- Memoirs of a Geisha

- Anthony Bourdain Parts Unknown: S8E6, S6E3, S2E7

- Kill Bill: Volume 1

- Tokyo!

Welcome to Japan

Arriving in Japan

Upon departing the airport, you will need to find transportation to your accommodations or other destination. My advice for each international point of arrival is below:

- **Tokyo Narita to Tokyo** (City): Reserve a ticket on the Narita Express to get into Tokyo for around 40 USD (4k Yen). This will take you from Narita Airport to the various main hubs in the Tokyo Metro area such as Tokyo Station, Shinjuku, Shibuya, Shinagawa and Yokohama, which takes no more than 1-1.5 hours. You will need to purchase a reserved seat on this train in the station. My advice: Skip trying to figure out where to do this yourself in the station and ask the staff.

- **Tokyo Narita to Tokyo Haneda Airport**: If you happen to be catching a connecting domestic flight upon arrival, you'll likely need to transfer to Haneda Airport, in the Southern area of Tokyo. To do this: Exit the customs area and look for the "Airport Limousine" counter and take the transfer bus to Haneda. Expect around 2 hours of travel time.

- **Haneda to Tokyo** (City): Take either of the 2 local lines available at Haneda, the Keikyu *(kay-que)* line to various stops in the city, or the Monorail direct to Hamamatsucho Station, where you can access the

Yamanote *(yama-no-tay)* line which circles the city. Also, the Limousine Bus, which has a counter outside of arrivals, makes stops at each of the major stations in Tokyo, which may be more convenient with the exception of during rush hour.

- **Kansai Airport to Osaka**: Kansai Airport in Osaka is located about 1-hour Southeast from the city itself. Upon arrival, there is only 1 train (local train) available to get to the city. This will take you to Osaka Station, where you can make your way to anywhere else in the city or catch the Shinkansen elsewhere at Shin-Osaka Station, just a short local train or taxi from Osaka Station (they are two different stations).

- **Fukuoka International Airport:** A relatively small airport, exit the airport and catch the bus to Hakata train station and bus terminal. From here you can get anywhere in the region, including via the Shinkansen and the Limited Express train to the Nagasaki area.

- **Central Japan Airport** (Nagoya): Catch the local train to Nagoya Station in about 30 minutes. From here you can get anywhere in the region, including the via Shinkansen.

Lockers and Luggage Services

You may find yourself in a situation where it is inconvenient to cart your luggage with you, either during the day or from city to city. There are 2 options to deal with this:

- Lockers sized from small to large enough to fit a suitcase into can be found at nearly every airport or train station. I highly recommend using these in the event you don't need to drag your luggage around with you. These can be paid by small bills or by the IC Card. For IC card use, you must pick the luggage up with the same IC card. Also, ensure that you keep the receipt. If you try to pick up your luggage and have lost either one, you'll be in a very bad position. Keep it safe.

- **Black Cat or *Kuroneko*.** Officially Yamato Transport, I cannot recommend this service enough. This is a delivery service that operates throughout the country which has pickup/ drop-off points located everywhere. Additionally, they can pick-up your luggage at your hotel, and have it delivered to a hotel, airport or Black Cat location in another city within 24-48 hours. Black Cat can also utilize most convenience stores as drop-off/ pick-up locations, but this requires a native Japanese speaker to help coordinate these more complex details. This service is great for avoiding transporting your luggage on trains. Simply drop your luggage off at the Black Cat location in the airport, provide the drop-off location, and your luggage will arrive when estimated, like clockwork. You can also schedule a hotel pickup online.

Japanese Police

Japanese police are a strange breed. Given the low crime rate, it seems they get easily bored, and sometimes show up in force to otherwise non-important situations. On the other hand, they seem to not care too much about crimes between foreigners, or crimes against foreigners, unless it turns into a political situation where they must act to save embarrassment. Believe it or not, the police usually have a general balance or understanding with the organized crime groups as long as order is maintained, and everyday Japanese citizens aren't caught up in criminal matters (i.e. Grandma isn't robbed and shot by a drunk Yakuza). Best to not get them involved in anything unless absolutely necessary.

If, however, you happen to lose an item while out and about, check with the local police outpost called a "koban," which are usually located near train stations. Miraculously, lost items are commonly found and returned to the nearest koban, due to the general good nature most Japanese people have. This is the only interaction with Japanese police you should have.

Laws

While in Japan, assume that most laws from your home apply here as well. What may be different, however, is how strictly the Japanese population follows each and every law, no matter how seemingly stupid or insignificant.

Below are just a few odd-balls that you may easily break without knowing it, or some that seem small in your country but could get you talking to the police rather quickly in Japan.

- **Jaywalking:** The easiest one to break. Wait for the crosswalk signal before walking. Not only will this possibly save you from a jaywalking ticket handed out by the bored police force, but the other people waiting are very likely to blindly follow you across the street, including that 90-year old woman who can't walk fast enough to avoid the bus. Given the highly obedient nature of most Japanese people, they will assume that it is okay to cross if someone else is crossing (it's a strange phenomenon). Don't be the leader of a group of people that got hit by a bus.

- **Littering:** Not even a cigarette butt. Though you will not get whipped to death, it looks very disrespectful and is enforced.

- **Trash Separation:** Trash receptacles are separated by type of trash, so take note of that as well. You'd be amazed how offensive not doing this can be to people.

- **Drugs:** No drugs are legal in Japan, to include opioid pain meds and some prescription and OTC drugs. Drug laws are strictly enforced in Japan. If caught, it will not be a smack on the hand or a fine. You will spend many years of your life eating fish heads and rice. Japanese prison is not a fun place to be.

- **Fighting:** Don't get into a fight, especially with Japanese people. Best case is the police will have no problem locking up a violent foreigner any day of the week. Worst case is the local Yakuza faction gets involved.

- **Smoking:** Don't smoke outside of smoking areas. Smoking is allowed practically everywhere except outside on the streets or sidewalks.

- **Drinking and Driving:** If you will be renting a car in Japan, you should know the blood alcohol level is 0.03%. This means that one drink, even hours before driving, will get you a DUI. Oh, and a DUI will land you in jail.

- **Trains:** Don't sit in the priority seats or stand in the "Ladies Only' trains.

Dining and Drinking

Truthfully, the dining and drinking culture of Japan is what most people enjoy the most. Japanese people put their heart and soul into their work, and an outcome of this is a country full of culinary experiences and tastes that are almost not of this world. This is where all business deals and personal relationships are started. In Japan, you don't know someone until you've eaten a meal and drank with them, and this is a key aspect of Japan you must understand.

Tokyo alone is home to 501 Michelin rated restaurants and literally millions of other places to dine. Listed below are some of the most popular types of food and dining experiences you're surely going to want to try while in the country:

- **Theme Restaurants**: Though not too popular outside of Tokyo, Japan has hundreds of dining establishments that have an entire décor, menu and staff entertainment experience that correlates to a certain place and time or another theme, from a haunted hospital to a ninja-themed restaurant. They even have a place where you dine in the nude, in complete darkness, to heighten your taste senses. We will mention a few in the Tokyo chapter.

- **Teppanyaki** *(tep-in-yaki)*: Steak houses where a fabulous meal is prepared in front of you on a hibachi grill. Think Benihana but authentic.

- **Izakaya** *(is-a-ka-ya)*: Popular across the entire country, this favorite of workplace gatherings and social events commonly have a "set" course, where you can eat various types of food and drink all you want for a set price. Dishes come in larger portions and are meant to be shared. Think of these like an all you can eat appetizer restaurant. I still don't see how these places make money, and it is a great way to sample many foods and drink your heart out for a low price. Look for the ones that advertise a yen amount, next to either a 2 or 3. This would mean "XXXX yen for

X hours" of time. (This may require a Japanese friend for translation/ordering).

- **Sushi:** We all know what sushi is. In Japan, there are many types of sushi restaurants:

  A. Sushi go-arounds: Premade sushi dishes are presented on a rotating conveyor that you can pick from as it passes your table. Keep the dish, it's how they tally your bill.

  B. Conveyor belt style: Order from an iPad-like controller and the sushi is sent out via conveyor to your table. Most will have an English option, and you need to choose "Tabulate Bill" when you are finished.

  C. Traditional: Sit at the bar and order from the sushi chef directly, or a table. These may or may not have English menus, so ask before you sit down to avoid an awkward moment. (See Translation section)

  Sushi Tips:

  1) *Most sushi restaurants have green tea and a hot water spout at the table. Do not burn yourself.*

  2) *Do not order a specialty roll. That includes the California kind. They're not Japanese.*

- **Yakiniku** (*ya-kee-nee-koo*): My personal favorite. Known in other countries as Korean BBQ, but much better in Japan. Your table will have either a charcoal or gas grill in the center, where you can grill small pieces of premium meat and vegetables right at your table. Usually, the meats available will be very high quality and locally sourced Kobe Beef or Wagyu. Best enjoyed with many cold beers. *Note: Do not grill the bacon with other meat on the grill. Great way to start a fire or burn yourself. Such scenarios and the liability they present are why we cannot enjoy this experience outside of Japan.

- **Ramen:** Not like you'll find in the grocery aisle. Each city has its own style, and slurping is encouraged. A staple of any Japanese diet and late-night alcohol sponge. Make sure to order Gyoza as well, because Ramen without Gyoza is like a burger without fries.

- **Okonomiyaki** (*oh-ko-no-mee-yaki*): A type of noodle pancake pressed with cabbage, fried egg and your choice of seafood or pork, made on a hibachi grill in front of you. The Okonomiyaki sauce completes the dish and is best enjoyed topped with mayo and a cold beer. Popular in Osaka and Hiroshima.

- **Yakitori** (*yak-ee-toe-ree*): Grilled skewers of chicken parts and other foods. I do mean "parts." Sit and order directly from the cook at the bar if you can, provided an English menu. Order "yakitori" and you'll probably get the chicken parts you are familiar with. Pointing and nodding is also an accepted way to order.

- **Tempura:** Lightly battered and fried everything, but in a healthy way. Literally, everything comes in tempura. Order a tempura set and you'll get a nice variety of fish, chicken, squid and native veggies. Stir the provided radish into the sauce for dipping.

- **Shabu:** A hot pot of flavored broths in the center of the table for stewing slices of meat and veggies. Comes with a variety of flavors.

As it is good to know the types of food and experiences you will encounter, you also need to know a few things to help you along the process to save you from embarrassment:

1) When entering, if you receive the sign of crossed arms, this means they are full, have no English menu and can't communicate or you are not welcome for another reason. Don't argue, just move along.

2) You will be asked how many in your party, to which a show of fingers is acceptable.

3) It is prudent to ask for an English menu or "eigo menu" before being seated. If there is a negative reaction, choose your next move wisely and ascertain how much you'll bother them if you stay.

4) Take off your shoes. Where the hardwood transitions to carpet or other material is an indication of the "no shoe" zone. Most nicer places provide a small locker at the entrance for your shoes.

5) The majority of restaurants have a call button at the table, usually located near the condiments or ashtrays (yes you can smoke inside most places

in Japan). This is how you call the wait staff, but do not abuse it. Call button abuse is why other cultures are incapable of mastering this genius method of service.

6) If there is no button, you may call the wait staff by calling out "Sumimasen" (*soo-mee-ma-sin*) which directly means "pardon me." If not heard, don't yell, have a Japanese person or a woman say it (the tone makes the difference).

7) Many smaller restaurants and Ramen shops have vending machine ordering systems which can be confusing to use. These are located at the entrance and you must pay, make a selection and receive a ticket prior to entry. To use these, place your money in as you normally would, select your meal (most have a photo on the selection button) and take your ticket to the staff.

8) If dining with Japanese people, wait until everyone has their food or drink before partaking in yours. Once all drinks are received, proper cheers or "Kampai" (*kum-pie*) can be had, making sure to touch everyone's glass, before drinking.

9) When someone pours your drink, accept the pour by raising your glass with your right hand only, while holding your lower right arm with your left hand. Respond by pouring the offerors drink for them on the next round, with both hands. This goes on until everyone is fairly drunk, don't worry it's the culture and part of socializing. If a guest, you'll receive

this as long as your glass is empty, so drink slow if you don't want to become drunk.

10) Do not stick chopsticks into food vertically. This is a bad omen related to funerals and death. Rest your chopsticks horizontally on your plate, bowl or on the provided holder.

11) If you are alone, don't ask for a 4-person table. Sit at the bar.

12) Do not even attempt to separate the bill. The ensuing confusion will be brutal. Figure it out internally.

13) Pay at the register near the door. Do not pay at the table. Read the section on Money.

A night of bonding over a meal and drinks is sure to win you new friends in Japan and usually leads to an even better time after the meal. Japanese people are very friendly, and any offers of additional gatherings should be accepted readily. You never know where your new friends could take you that you would have had no chance of going on your own.

Tipping

Tipping is not customary in Japan, and staff will not allow you to tip. They will return your money to you. Do not try to tip, even if you have received the best service imaginable. It is actually slightly insulting. The reason for this lies in the ingrained Japanese desire to do ones' absolute best at their work, or at least appear to be doing so. So, tipping may suggest the possibility that at other times, less than 100% effort is given or may alienate other staff. See how that works?

Nightlife in Japan

"Pity the salaryman. Tokyo's willing cog in an enormous machine requiring long hours, low pay, total dedication and sometimes...death by overwork. But at night...things are different."

-Anthony Bourdain

The country that invented the concept of "work hard, play hard," the overworked locals are world famous for their ability to let it all out at night. Saying that Japan has amazing nightlife is like saying that Israel and Palestine aren't friendly to one another. It's so much more complex. There is literally so much to do, that if you went out every night of your life, you'd need multiple lives to do all there is to do… and that's only Tokyo. Japan's nightlife areas put every other country's equivalent to shame (and I've been to many). Between the multitudes of restaurants and the infinite entertainment options beyond that, a night owl will never get bored here, assuming a supportive budget. Japan can be costly for even the most seasoned and well-heeled party animal.

Trendy bars, hole in the wall bars, live rock music, candlelit cocktail lounges, Irish or English pubs, DJ rooms, disco, dance clubs, hostess clubs, and cabaret shows, all can be found within the same few blocks in most major cities and their smaller neighborhoods. All this among the same areas as thousands of different restaurants, karaoke complexes, and hotels.

Nightlife in Japan is clearly a subject requiring a book all its own. We will cover the major cities and the most famous nightlife areas, but below are some general guidelines and expectations:

- Drinking in Japan is how people of all walks of life bond and socialize, but when the work gatherings end and salarymen head to the trains, the late-night shenanigans are just beginning.

- Drinking in public is not only legal in Japan, but it is also highly common for groups to gather in parks and sip on beer or drinks from the convenience store before heading off for the night.

- Since trains stop at midnight, most clubs don't get going until after that and most late-nighters won't be heading home until the trains start again at 5:00 am, though this applies mainly to Tokyo and Osaka.

- It is common to see local salarymen sleeping/ drunkenly passed out on the street. They are not homeless, they simply missed the train. Please leave them be.

- Bring plenty of cash and try not to use your credit card. Most establishments are cash only and some bigger clubs have been known to run up the bill or extort you in some of the seedier areas of Tokyo.

- Be wary of the street touts inviting you into certain places with promises of a good time or discount. The more aggressive their tactics, the less likely you should be to take them up on their offer. Again, this applies mostly to Tokyo.

- The famous tall neon signs on the buildings above the streets are the signs for the bars within that building. Yeah, there are that many. Some of the most fun you can have is by exploring these places but be prepared to not be allowed into many. But… it may be worth finding that needle in the haystack.

- Go out with Japanese friends. If you don't have any, try your best to make some. Doors will open for you that were closed before and you'll have a much better time.

- There is something for everyone and every niche, fad or style imaginable.

Convenience Stores

Convenience stores or "Conbini" (*cone-beanie*) in Japan are fabulous. Forget what you know from back home, you will find no 3-day old hot dogs or rude clerks here. What you WILL find are anything and everything you could possibly ever need. This includes:

- Toiletries, cleaning supplies, medicines, umbrellas, toilet paper, paper towels,

- Electronics such as phone chargers, batteries and other various things you didn't know you needed until you didn't have it;

- Magazines, all sorts of interesting magazines can be found here;

- Drinks, to include beer, liquor, and chu-his, delicious but dangerously strong and highly popular fruit-flavored spirits in a can. They even have a great selection of hangover prevention drinks (look for the turmeric on the can). Grab some drinks here and save some money before going out for the night.

- Food, both the expected chips and candy variety (though much more interesting) as well as many varieties of fresh food, and prepared meals that only need to be heated, which is done in the store. Masses of workers in Japan get their lunch or dinner each day from convenience stores, so you know it must be good. You must explore the conbini food options or you've missed a big part of Japan.

- Money. As mentioned, you will be getting your money from 711 or Family Mart most of the time.

- Toilets. If out and about, most convenience stores have clean and available restrooms for public use.

Vending Machines

In the very uncommon scenario that you are unable to find a convenience store when in need, don't worry. Vending machines are even more common than conbini. For every 1 conbini, there must be 1,000 vending machines in this country, and not only containing soft drinks. These are scattered all over the place, to include in front yards and at random points on the side of the road. They are both cooled and heated, the blue and red colored spaces indicating which, and many accept IC cards. Some things you can find include:

- Drinks including coffee, tea, water, juices, soft drinks and energy drinks;

- Cigarettes, beer and sometimes chuhis and canned whiskey and coke;

- Ice cream, canned soups, and other snacks; and

- Strange items that should never be found in a vending machine which we should not and will not discuss here.

Must Do Activities:

There are certain activities that all visitors absolutely must do while in Japan, to get the full experience. Ask anyone who has spent time in the country, and I guarantee you that they will agree.

- **Karaoke:** I don't care who you are, or how terrible of a singer you are, find a way to make some Japanese friends and spend an hour or two in a karaoke box. Karaoke complexes in Japan are more comparable in appearance and function to a hotel than anything else. A multi-level building with numerous small rooms, complete with large TV and party lights, sound system, and a phone to order on-demand food and drinks. Karaoke is also popular with aging salarymen at hostess clubs, but it's not the best time. Either way, best enjoyed with Japanese friends.

- **Japanese Baseball:** The Japanese love baseball, and they get very into the games. A great time if you have the chance and plentiful with food and drink. You'll love the beer maids, carrying mini-kegs of beer on their backs serving it cold on the spot and the coordinated chants they have for each player.

- **Sumo:** Attend a Sumo match. These are held in the largest cities at differing times of the year and deserve to be on your list: Tokyo in January, May, September; Osaka in March and Fukuoka in November. If not traveling then, you can also visit one of the Sumo stables in Tokyo, many of which are located in the Asakusa area. Here you can get close and really experience it.

- **Hanami** (*ha-na-mee*)**:** The annual cherry blossom blooming in April. A time-honored celebration that lasts briefly each year and symbolizes the short time we have on earth. Fun time complete with outdoor BBQs, beer and friends.

- **Summer Festivals:** If visiting in the summer, festivals are held in every town and city throughout Japan. Complete with fireworks, food stalls, street marching, cultural performances and the like. This is where the entire population dresses in traditional summertime Yukata, and some of the fireworks held are the best you'll ever see. One of the best things about living in Japan. Do be warned that accommodations get pricey in the large cities and crowds are no joke.

- **Temples:** Japan is not short of Temples, and you'll surely be seeing many of them. Most are incredibly old and represent this rich culture like nothing else really can. There is no one destination for temples (though one could be forgiven for saying Kyoto) , you'll find theme everywhere you go.

- **Onsens:** Japan is full of volcanic activity, and one of the benefits is the abundance of hot springs. Most popular in Winter time, a visit to an Onsen (hot spring) should be high on your list. There are public and private onsens, and hotels dedicated to onsens. You may need to travel a bit and it may be pricey, but entirely worth it for the experience, not to mention the water is supposedly high in all sorts of good nutrients. The Oita region East of Fukuoka on the Southern island of Kyushu are the most famous onsen areas in Japan, with the town of Beppu being the pinnacle.

You'll need to ensure that you follow the rules at any Onsen. Mainly:

1. No visible tattoos are allowed. They may allow you in with a covering or shirt.

2. Bathe/shower before entering the Onsen. They're for soaking, not bathing.

3. Obey the segregation rules. Public Onsens are typically gender segregated.

- **Mount Fuji:** I recommend at least a visit to get up close. Japan's highly regarded spiritual mountain, many climbers flock to the top each year to make the 2 to 3-day trek to the 10,000-foot summit. Don't go in the winter. If you decide to hike it, plan for 3 days minimum.

- **Sake Tasting:** A visit to a local sake factory is always a nice time. Japan has many types of sake from all over the country, each with its own distinct character.

- **Toyosu Fish Market:** Formerly the Tsukiji Fish Market, and the largest in the world, where all fish enters the Tokyo area each day to be distributed through the city and surrounding regions. You'll need to be there before dawn though, as the fish needs to get to its destinations in time for lunch.

- **Beer Gardens:** Another summertime tradition, Beer Gardens can be found atop many of the department stores and hotels in the cities. Similar to an open-air buffet with grills right at your table, a great pastime for winding down from the week with friends and coworkers before hitting some karaoke.

- **Skiing/Boarding:** Hokkaido and Nagano are world famous destinations for winter sports. Also, the Japanese are very into it and there's a big winter sports culture, so it's a great time.

- **Halloween:** If you are up for a party and in Japan during Halloween, make your way to Tokyo or Osaka, where they take it very seriously. I would compare Halloween in these Japanese cities to Mardi Gras in New Orleans. Where you can really take advantage of those foreigner stereotypes.

- **Arcades:** Everyone is familiar with the popularity of video game culture in Japan. Besides being the birthplace of Nintendo, and every video game cult classic since then, the cult following is HUGE here. Arcades in Japan can occupy entire 10 story buildings, packed with hundreds, if not thousands, of video game-obsessed youth, at all hours of the day and night. And they aren't just playing your average run of the mill games either, there is really some fascinating stuff going on you need to check out, at minimum, to observe how big of a phenomenon it is. Some say this is also a major contributor to the declining birth rate in the country but, who am I to say.

The Rules

Now, this is why you really bought this book. Before we dive into my specific recommendations for certain cities, I have compiled a list of things to make sure you **DO** and also **DON'T** do to make sure:

- Your experience is as smooth as possible
- You avoid international incidents, arrest or otherwise offend your Japanese hosts

These things have been learned over the course of my extensive time in Japan, through many relationships with Japanese people and a very busy social calendar. If you heed this advice, you should have no problem making new friends in Japan, who may even take it upon themselves to show you a really great time considering what a good person you seem to be.

<u>DO</u>

- Observe and mimic the locals. If they aren't doing it, you probably shouldn't do it either.

- Take off your shoes when entering a home, dining or other personal areas.

- Respond to any bow-like gesture or head-nod in like kind. Not doing so will be highly offensive. This is not a show of submission or dominance, it is a show of mutual respect and will go a very long way.

- Refrain from touching or hugging people that you have not gotten to know. Handshakes are acceptable but not common.

- Be patient and remain calm in your everyday dealings.

- Make Japanese friends to go out with. Best way to experience Japan.

- Pour others' drinks when they pour yours.

- Wait for others to get their drinks or food before partaking.

- Place cash or credit card in the small tray at any point of sale. That's what it is there for.

- Accept a Japanese business card with both hands and spend 5 seconds looking at it.

- Refer to people you meet with a "san" at the end of their last name. In informal settings, this can be relaxed for younger Japanese people, but never for those older than you. To play it safe, always use **LAST NAME-san** until you've become more acquainted. Never use the first name only when meeting.

- Ask permission or confirm that it is ok prior to making yourself at home at any establishment.

- Wait in line. You will never see Japanese people mob or cut in line. You should do the same.

- Give your train seat to women and elderly people. Don't be a jerk.

- Carry plenty of cash and use the change as it accrues.

- Check to ensure your payment method is acceptable prior to placing an order if using a card.

- Drink responsibly, and avoid being slipped drugs, especially in the nightlife areas of Roppongi, Shinjuku, and Shibuya.

- Wait for the crosswalk signal before walking.

- Look for the **RED** light in the taxis, not the **GREEN**.

DO NOT

- Talk loudly on public transportation, restaurants or in any public setting where you are the loudest person around. This includes phone calls.

- Smoke in public areas or on the street.

- Sneeze or cough without a mask. Those masks you see people wearing mean THEY are sick and politely not spreading. Not the other way around. Sneezing or coughing will draw you the ire of those around you if you have no mask.

- Stick chopsticks into food vertically.

- Rest your feet up on seats or other furniture items.

- Enter establishments when enticed to do so by other foreigners in Roppongi.

- Use your credit or debit card at a nightclub or bar in Roppongi or Shinjuku.

- Expect to use your credit card at all establishments.

- Take the Tokyo and Osaka Metro trains during rush hour if it can be avoided.

- Eat on public transportation.

- Carry 10,000 yen notes and expect change.

- Keep money wadded or crumpled unless you want to offend almost anyone you give money to.

- Enter Onsens, waterparks, pools or public baths with tattoos visible. This is very taboo, and they must be covered.

- Refer to someone by their first name only.

- Fight or argue. Just create distance and move along if instigated.

- Bring up anything related to World War 2. Unless you have gotten to know someone very well and want to have an intelligent conversation in a respectful manner, the odds are great that bringing this topic up will backfire on you. The term "sore subject" comes to mind.

Tokyo

"What do you need to know about Tokyo? Deep, deep waters."

-Anthony Bourdain

Where to even begin. As Japan's (and the world's) largest city and the point of entry for the great majority of visitors, Tokyo is the obvious starting point for this book. Tokyo is a mega-city, made up of numerous sub-cities, each with its own character and history. One could really spend their entire life exploring Tokyo and barely scratch the surface. It truly is a vast urban wilderness, a three-dimensional maze of the unknown, chock full of experiences that are best explored by just getting out there and taking it all in. Sensory overload is a term that comes to mind when I think about what it must be like for first-time visitors. So, with that said, I hope I can provide some guidance grounded in my extensive experience that will assist you along the way in your quest to experience Japan's most interesting and overwhelming city. For the purposes of this book, we will not go into the level of detail about Tokyo that it deserves. Insider Tokyo information is the subject of many books much longer than 40 minutes. For a more detailed, yet concise, guide of Tokyo, pick up my other book **Tokyo: An Insider's Guide for the Savvy Traveler.**

Getting Around

Firstly, below are all mandatory items for getting around and exploring Tokyo, whether during the day or night:

- Phone service

- Ample phone charge with external charging capability (preferably a charger case or mobile charging device)

- Hyperdia mobile app

- Suica AND Pasmo IC Cards (covers all trains, buses, and taxis)

- Patience and the ability to overcome crowd anxiety, or at least the ability to prepare for it

The reasons for this are, simply, that mapping your way through Tokyo is a heavy drain on your phone, as you will be constantly referencing a map, app or googling your next destination. Be prepared and do not get into a situation where you are dead in the water due to navigation or phone related issues. A day and night out in Tokyo will easily consume 200% of a fully-charged iPhone battery.

The Tokyo train system will likely be the first (and worst) overwhelming obstacle you experience in Japan. Due to years of expansion, renovation, the addition of numerous train lines and more expansion, many of Tokyo's stations are a mess of long corridors, stairs, dead ends, confusing signage and more comparable to a bowl of tangled Ramen noodles than an organized transportation hub. You can be walking towards a train track, then realize there are numerous tracks of the same number, or even find yourself in an underground mall that seemingly came out of nowhere. This can be incredibly confusing even while using every technology aid possible, even for the locals.

Be prepared to need to exit one station, walk 5 minutes down the street, and enter another station to make connections. Do not rely simply on your navigational instincts or the general idea that since your destination is North, you should take XX line to XX because that is also North. I cannot stress enough the use of Hyperdia or even Google Maps Transit feature to aid you in navigating Tokyo's train system. **My advice?** When the slightest doubt enters your mind about if you are on the right path, ask the station staff for assistance on where to go for your connecting train. Many speak English and may even be kind enough you walk you personally to the correct track. This will save you time and possibly even prevent you from getting on the wrong train. Tokyo's train system is quite an adventure.

Tokyo Navigation Tips:

- *Get Hyperdia. If you're too cheap, use Google Maps Transit feature.*
- *Buy Suica and Pasmo Cards. Keep them charged up with money (done at the point of sale).*
- *Do NOT take large luggage on the train. Use the Black Cat service*
- *Avoid trains at rush hour (8-9:00 am, 5-7:00 pm)*

- *Take a snapshot of your itinerary on Hyperdia or Google Maps for reference while on the train. Phone service is scarce in the subways and it will save your battery.*

- *Reference the train platform signage on the columns and walls before getting on/ off the train.*

- *When you don't see a sign for what you're looking for, ask someone. You're probably off course.*

- *When taking luggage on a train (IF you must), keep in mind that the exit doors can change sides without warning. Try to stay in a neutral location so you can exit at either side if needed.*

Aside from the trains, most of the traveling you will do will be on foot. Since train stations are scattered literally all over the city, it is rare that you will walk more than 500 meters without coming across a train station. Taxis and the high cost can easily be avoided if you aren't in a rush.

Where to Stay

As opposed to other cities, where you stay in Tokyo will be highly dependent on what you plan on doing. My in depth article on the Tokyo neighborhoods and where to stay is a must-read at www.40minutetravelguru.com

Neighborhoods

Tokyo has 23 different wards and 47 different neighborhoods, each with its own character, quirks, history, demographics and things it seems to be famous for. The ones you will likely want to see as a tourist are listed below.

Shinjuku

One of the main nightlife, business, and transportation hubs in Tokyo, Shinjuku *(shin-joo-ku)* is a city all its own. Besides claiming the title of "World's Busiest Train Station" at 2 million people per day, the area around Shinjuku Station is bustling with a unique combination of restaurants, shopping, nightlife and attractions that is second to none in Tokyo. For the majority of restaurants and entertainment, you will want to stick around the Kabukicho (*Ka-bookee-cho)* area, just to the East-Northeast of the main train station. This area is one of the main entertainment hubs of Tokyo and is popular with the 20 something crowds as well as the working-class adults. In addition, Shinjuku is also home to many government buildings, office parks, high-end hotels, and some very nice museums and parks, all discussed below.

Shibuya

Just south of Shinjuku on the JR Yamanote line, Shibuya is a highly popular shopping, dining and nightlife hub. Most recognized worldwide by the insanely congested intersection outside of Shibuya station (the most highly foot-trafficked crosswalk in the world), Shibuya is one of the most popular neighborhoods in Tokyo for the 20 to 30 something crowds, with its youthful energy and plethora of shopping, food, and entertainment.

Roppongi

Known for its shopping, art galleries, beautiful high-rise office buildings and yet almost stigmatized by its world-famous reputation for wild and somewhat seedy nightlife, it's hard to think of Tokyo without thinking of Roppongi. By far the most popular area in the city for foreign tourists and expats, this truly international business district by day/ party district by night is a must visit. Classy and professional during the day, hosting the Tokyo offices of many multinationals such as Google and Goldman Sachs, this area gets wild after the sun goes down.

Ueno

Located just north of Tokyo Station, Ueno is most notable for its museums, parks and the Ueno zoo, home to the wildly popular Panda exhibit. In fact, within Ueno Park is where most of Tokyo's best museums can be found and is visited by millions of visitors each year. Historically a working-class neighborhood, and certainly worthy of a spot in your daytime sightseeing agenda, I do not recommend staying around Ueno due to the lack of notable nightlife or dining, compared to other Tokyo neighborhoods, and its rough reputation amongst the locals.

Ginza

Tokyo's uber-wealthy center for shopping, "The Ginza" is to Tokyo what upper 5th Avenue is to New York. Primarily a shopping destination and some of the most expensive real estate in the world, Ginza is also host to some of the most expensive restaurants and best architecture in the city. If you decide to visit for a daytime shopping trip, it's worth a stay into the evening even if only to see the famous Ginza lights along the strip.

Asakusa

East of Tokyo Station, the "Old Town" of Asakusa is most known for the Senso-Ji Temple, and the numerous shopping streets in the surrounding area. Though not especially notable for dining or nightlife (Asakusa is eerily quiet at night), I would recommend a visit here.

Akasaka

Not to be confused with Asakusa, Akasaka is located just East of Roppongi. A bit of a nightlife center in its own regard, Akasaka is host to an abundant number of hotels from which you could base yourself in your explorations of the other parts of the city. A bit more upscale than Roppongi, and certainly fewer foreigners, but not quite Ginza.

Akihabara

The place to find anime, arcades, manga and maid cafes, and giant electronics stores. Worth a daytime stop at minimum. Truly the anime and electronics capital of Tokyo, and therefore the world.

Ebisu

International feel, yet quiet and filled with cafes, restaurants, and bars. Ebisu is just 3-5 minutes via train from both Shibuya and Roppongi but has a very residential feel to it. You could easily stay here and enjoy it or venture out and back without much trouble.

Odaiba

A manmade island in Tokyo Bay, home to a few parks such as the Odaiba Seaside Park, famous museums and some very nice Architecture. Accessible via train or the Rainbow bridge, but also via ferry from Asakusa, Odaiba makes for a nice daytime retreat if the weather is nice, or a nice overnight stay.

Harajuku

The epicenter of cute anime style fashion, and other whacky youth fashion trends of the day, in Japan known as *"Kawaii"* which directly translates to "cute," but really represents an entire youth fashion movement. A stroll through Harajuku amongst the masses dressed out in "Harajuku Style" will absolutely make you feel like you're trapped in a Japanese teenage girl's dream.

<u>Jimbocho</u>

Known for its art galleries and coffee shops. You can find some very nice art here it that's your thing

What to Eat

Tokyo is home to 501 Michelin star rated restaurants, so this is not a complete list. Tens of thousands of amazing experiences await. These are just a few of my favorites.

- **Maguro Shouten** (Shinjuku): Tuna Demolition show
- **Robot Restaurant** (Shinjuku): Lavish show including girls in bikinis and robots. Must see.
- **Samurai Restaurant** (Shinjuku)
- **The Lockup** (Shinjuku): Haunted prison theme.
- **Zauo Fishing Restaurant** (Shinjuku): Catch your dinner.
- **Hakushu Teppenyaki** (Shibuya): Hibachi steak.
- **Gonpachi** (Roppongi): Kill Bill fight scene restaurant.
- **Sushi Sukiyabashi Jiro** (Roppongi): Most expensive sushi in Japan.
- **Roppongi Hills:** Not a restaurant, but the highest concentration of dining in Roppongi.

- **Uka-tei** (Ginza): Teppanyaki restaurant at the top of the Chanel building. Expensive and worth it.

- **Bulgari Tokyo** (Ginza): Located on the top floor of the Bulgari store, Italian food with a view.

- **Bird Land Ginza** (Ginza): All things chicken, on skewers. High rated *Yakitori.*

Nightlife

Easily the world's most vivid and amazing nightlife, each area of Tokyo has its own entertainment district that alone would rival most major cities. A night out in Tokyo for the first timer will leave you amazed and open your eyes to a world you didn't know existed. I will highlight the major areas.

- **Kabukicho** (Shinjuku): The entertainment area is not only home to world-class entertainment and restaurants, but also contains many "red-light" establishments co-mingled with thousands of entertainment establishments with nothing to do with the red-light industry. A stroll through here will overload the senses with food shops, hostess and host clubs, pubs, live music venues, cabarets, and strip clubs.

- **Golden Gai** (Shinjuku): A famous street where various small bars are located, this street contains many small, and sometimes cramped, bars, each with its own catch.

- **Roppongi:** Tokyo's seedy party capital. The areas surrounding Roppongi crossing are known to be the wildest nightlife in Tokyo with 100's of pubs, dance clubs, DJ clubs, hostess clubs, cabaret shows and everything in between. Easily the most visited nightlife area by foreigners, make sure you don't start a tab anywhere here and think twice before being led into a bar by a street advertiser. A fun place but you must not let your guard down.

- **Shibuya/ Dogenzaka:** In addition to the plethora of dining options that can and will carry you on into the night, Shibuya has a thriving nightclub and bar scene, rivaling Roppongi as a nightclub destination. Not nearly as seedy as some areas in Shinjuku or Roppongi, plenty of fun can be had in the nightclubs and bar areas around Dogenzaka and the West side of the station after dark. As with anywhere else, best enjoyed simply wandering to see what you can find.

- **Asakusa:** Asakusa is a less foreigner populated nightlife area, with a focus more on dining and cocktail lounges that close before the night gets too late. Close to Roppongi.

While out and about in Tokyo, I highly recommend you observe these ***Cardinal Rules*** for Tokyo nightlife to be especially observed in Roppongi and Shinjuku:

1) *Do not enter establishments when enticed to do so by the foreigners working for the clubs on the street if they are pushy.*

2) *Leave your credit cards in your room and carry your wallet in your front pocket(s).*

3) *Never under any circumstance use your credit or debit card at a nightclub or bar in Roppongi or Shinjuku.*

4) *Drink responsibly and avoid being slipped drugs.*

5) *Remember, the trains stop at midnight and start again at 5:00 am.*

6) *Never buy or partake in any drug use.*

Attractions

- **Samurai Museum** (Shinjuku): Museum covering the history of the Samurai.

- **Shinjuku Gyoen National Garden** (Shinjuku): Famous outdoor lily pond and gardens, visit during the spring.

- **Yoyogi Park**: One of Tokyo's largest parks, Yoyogi is frequently hosting many festivals and a real escape from the madness that is Tokyo.

- **Meiji Jingu Shrine**: One of the most visited Shinto shrines, serenely secluded from the city in the northern part of Yoyogi Park.

- **Ueno Park**: Just west of Ueno Station lie Ueno park, the largest in Tokyo. Within the park are many museums, shrines, and the Ueno Zoo.

- **Ueno Zoo**: The largest zoo in Japan and notable for the Giant Panda exhibit.

- **Museums** (Ueno): A high concentration of amazing museums can be found in Ueno park.

- **Senso-Ji Temple** (Asakusa): One of the most visited temples in Japan, this area is rife with shopping stalls, souvenir shops, and small traditional eateries. Take a rickshaw ride around.

- **Tokyo Skytree** (Asakusa): The world's tallest tower, you can see every part of Tokyo and beyond on a clear day, to include Mount Fuji. Catch the sunset from here if you can.

- **Kabuki-za** (Ginza): Traditional Japanese theater, performed throughout the day and night. The best place to go in Tokyo for traditional "Kabuki" (theater).

- **Chuo Dori**: The main strip in Ginza. In addition to shopping, Chuo Dori is a must see after dark, as the lights are just amazing.

- **Imperial Palace**: The Imperial Palace is located just to the North of Ginza. Though the residence is not open to the public, tours of the palace ground and surrounding areas are available.

- **Tokyo Disney/ Disney Sea**: If you're coming from the US, I wouldn't worry about seeing this one. Very similar to Orlando, but if it's a family trip, worth considering. Expect heavy crowds here.

Tokyo Summary

You could spend your entire trip in only Tokyo, so for the scope of this book, my Tokyo section has been brief. If you want more information in a concise manner, with plenty of good insider info and links, pick up **Tokyo: An Insider's Guide for the Savvy Traveler.**

Osaka

Japans' 2nd largest city and my personal favorite, Osaka is similar to Tokyo only in the sheer number of things to do and see. The people are friendlier and known for their unique sense of humor, it's less congested, less confusing to get around, and a much more open feeling environment. Osaka is located on the East coast, about halfway between Hiroshima and Tokyo, and is easily accessible by both the Kansai International Airport and Shinkansen. Due to its abundant nightlife, many cultural sights, stunning architecture and position at the top of foodie's wish lists everywhere, Osaka should be on every Japan visitors' itinerary.

Getting Around

You will arrive into Osaka by either the Kansai Airport or the Shin-Osaka Station. Either way, you'll likely want to make your way to one of the main local train stations (Osaka, Umeda) in order to catch other local trains to your destination. Check your chosen transportation app for your specific needs. Beyond this, taxis are the only other means of public transportation in Osaka. All modes of transport accept the Icoca IC Card.

Where to Stay

The main hubs hosting a multitude of hotels, restaurants, shopping, and nightlife are the Umeda and Namba districts.

- **Umeda** (*oo-may-duh)*: Very near to Osaka and Shin-Osaka Stations, is the main train hub of the city and hosts higher-end hotels, shopping malls, restaurants, architecture, and other attractions. The urban "center" of Osaka. Distinguishable by the many skyscrapers and high-end hotels, Umeda is also host to lots of shopping and restaurant options located in and around Umeda Station. You could easily spend an entire afternoon and evening exploring this area.

- **Namba** (*nahm-ba)*: South of Umeda, is the area North of Namba Station and South of Shinsaibashi Station. Easily accessible via Namba Station, I recommend staying around here if you want to experience the vibrant nightlife and culinary experiences on offer in Osaka while being centrally located to be able to do plenty of sightseeing during the day. The Namba area is also home to Dotombori and Shinsaibashi neighborhoods, most famous for their vibrant nightlife and foods.

For comparison, Umeda is much busier during the day, while Namba gets very lively at night.

- Luxury: Hyatt, ANA Intercontinental, Hilton, Westin

- Mid-range: APA Hotels (scattered throughout Osaka), MyStays

- Love Hotel: The areas just West of Namba Station and Northeast of Nipponbashi Station are hosts to many Love Hotels. Worth a walkthrough at a minimum for the sheer shock factor.

What to Eat

Osaka is a world-famous culinary destination, literally packed with options for every type of food imaginable, both Japanese and foreign, cheap street food to gourmet 5-star restaurants, and some very interesting specialties specific to Osaka.

- **Takoyaki** is an Osaka staple, small bite-sized balls of batter with chopped octopus inside, flavored with ginger, onion and topped with a special Takoyaki sauce. These can be found at festivals and outdoor events all over Japan but are a "must eat" in Osaka.

- **Okonomiyaki.** Osaka is also famous for its version of Okonomiyaki which, in general, substitutes the noodles and cabbage found in Hiroshima style Okonomiyaki with a pancake batter. This can contain as many combinations of squid, shrimp, pork or oyster as you like. More similar to a pancake with added ingredients than Hiroshima style Okonomiyaki, ask any Japanese person which style they prefer, and they will surely have a strong opinion, similar to the Chicago deep dish vs. New York style pizza arguments in America. This is also a "must eat" and also cooked and served directly in front of you on a large hibachi style grill.

- The **Yakiniku** (Korean BBQ) offerings in Osaka are of especially high quality, due to the proximity to Kobe, the home of Kobe beef.

Nightlife

Osaka offers some of the best nightlife in Japan which, unsurprisingly, is located in and around Namba., to include the Dotombori and Shinsaibashi neighborhoods. Exit the Namba Station and head North, and you will hit the area around the Dotombori River canal, famous for its many lighted advertisements, shopping, and food stalls. Some of the best food in Osaka can be found around here simply by walking around and exploring the different options. I recommend the many canal side establishments for great food, drinks, and people watching. Some interesting shopping can also be had here, such as Don Quixote, and a number of nightclubs along the canal, as well as canal boat tours.

From Dotombori, Head just North across the canal and the Shinsaibashi neighborhood is home to hundreds upon hundreds of restaurants, nightclubs, bars, karaoke clubs and all sorts of entertainment options. People in Osaka are incredibly friendly and happy to help you find something to your liking. Unlike some parts of Tokyo, the invitations you may get from bar or club staff on the street are generally safe, though make sure you understand the club or bar "system" before entering to ensure you're not overpaying. If you can't have fun in Osaka, you're just not very fun.

- Foreigner/ Japanese Mix: Zero Bar, HUB, Balabushka
- Upscale/ Cocktails: Rooftop Bar OO, Absinthe

- Nightclub: Sam and Dave ONE

Attractions

- **Osaka Castle:** #1 on many visitors' lists, Osaka Castle is one of the larger castles in Japan and surely worth a visit. Originally built in the 16th century, the castle is surrounded by a scenic park and moat and requires at least 2-3 hours for a complete visit. There are some great views of the city from the top and the castle grounds are a popular place to enjoy the Hanami (cherry blossom season) in April of each year. The castle is also home to many summertime festivals. Access the castle via Osakajokoen Station nearby and be prepared for crowds.

- **Universal Studios Japan:** A very popular attraction for people all across Japan, Universal Studios Japan is similar to both the Orlando, FL and Hollywood, CA locations. Numerous special occasions/ festivals are held here throughout the year. Accessible via the Universal City train station. Just West of USJ and near the Osaka is the famous Tempozan Ferris wheel where you can enjoy some great views of the city.

- **Shitennoji Temple:** An ancient temple in the heart of Osaka. Not far from Namba Station and worth a stop.

- **Umeda:** Also discussed above, Umeda is the urban "center" of Osaka. Distinguishable by the many skyscrapers and high-end hotels, Umeda is also host to lots of shopping and restaurant options located in and around

Umeda Station. You could easily spend an entire afternoon and evening exploring this area.

- **Osaka Aquarium:** One of the largest aquariums in the world.

- **Sumo Tournaments:** Held each spring at the Osaka Prefectural Colosseum in Namba. Worth attending if your visit is timed right.

- **Bunraku Theater:** Traditional cultural shows and plays held regularly. Located in Nippombashi.

Kyoto

The capital of Japan for a thousand years, if you're coming to see the rich culture, tour ancient temples and hoping for a Geisha sighting, you must go to Kyoto. Home to 2,000 temples, shrines and Shinto holy sites, this must be on your list. If you simply Google search "Japan culture" I would think 70% of the images you see would be Kyoto. Oh, and those crowds I told you to avoid before? Yeah, they're going to Kyoto. But I won't dare tell you to avoid this amazing place.

Getting Around

Kyoto is one city that is easy to traverse from site to site on the bus system, which is the best way to do it if are sightseeing. Plenty of English sightseeing maps are available at Kyoto Station, where the bus hub is also located, and the bus system is very English friendly to accommodate the large numbers of foreign tourists who don't speak Japanese.

Where to Stay

Plenty of standard hotel options are available around Kyoto Station, but I recommend a stay at a traditional Japanese hotel or Ryokan here to fully experience the cultural feel of Japan. When in Kyoto, do as the Japanese.

- Luxury Ryokan: Hoshinoya Kyoto, Ryotei Rangetsu
- Mid-range Ryokan: Ryokufuso, Kyoto Ryokan Shoei

Additionally, the area around Kiyamachi-Dori (Kiyamachi Street) near the Geisha district of Gion is a fairly lively area if you want to be close to nightlife. This is the area just Northeast of Kawaramachi Station and runs parallel to the small river.

What to Eat

All of the best food from Japan can be had in Kyoto. For a night out of dining, I would head to Kiyamachi-Dori.

- **Kiyamachi Sakuragawa:** Traditional Japanese food in Kiyamachi
- **Chihaha:** Upscale Japanese food in Gion
- **Hatakaku:** Where a wild boar-based dish now popular in Japan was created, home of *Botan Nabe*. Located near the Imperial Palace.
- **Yoshikawa Tempura:** Former tearoom turned amazing Tempura, Sushi and Duck restaurant.

Nightlife

The Kiyamachi-Dori area is where Kyoto's nightlife is found. Not known as a nightlife city at all, you may be surprised how lively this area actually is. There is a vibrant bar and nightclub scene along the small river that can make for a good time.

- Foreigner/ Japanese Mix: HUB, Tun Tavern, Zaza Pub, Pig and Whistle
- Nightclub: Surfdisco, Butterfly, World, Ibiza

Attractions

As mentioned and as you know, there are simply too many must-see sites to list here. For more information on dining, nightlife and attractions in Kyoto, visit InsideKyoto.com.

Hiroshima

Hiroshima is Japans' 11th largest city located on the scenic Seto Inland Sea, in the middle of the main island of Honshu. When most hear the word "Hiroshima," they think of the A-Bomb dropped here at the end of World War 2 and the many lives lost. Today, Hiroshima is a bustling metropolis of 1.2M people, complete with (as of the time of writing) one of the best professional baseball teams, nightlife scenes and food cultures in the country. The city has come quite a long way since the destruction it saw in 1945 and seeing it while knowing that it has sprung up from complete ruin in barely 70 years is indeed impressive for first-time visitors. There is plenty to see in do in Hiroshima and it happens to be a city I know and adore.

Getting Around

Hiroshima has one mode of public transportation most other cities do not: Trollies. The Trollies serve in a similar fashion that the subways do (Hiroshima has no subway system). Exit the South side of the train station, and you will see the trollies platforms with maps of the city indicating which color line you should take to get to your destination. The Green line serves the city center. All modes of transport accept the Icoca IC Card.

Where to Stay

I recommend staying along the main thoroughfare through the city, Heiwa-Odori, just East of the Peace Park. This area is rife with shopping, restaurants, and nightlife and is easily accessible from the train station. The areas around the Parco mall are especially lively.

- Mid-range: Sheraton, Hotel Granvia, Rihga Royal

- Budget: Oriental, Washington, Sunroute

- Love Hotel: Bali Resort

What to Eat

Hiroshima is famous for 2 types of food: Oysters *(kaki)* and Okonomiyaki. The Oysters are farmed in the Seto Inland Sea, throughout the entire area. Most of the Oysters you find in Japan will likely have come from the Hiroshima area.

- **Okonomimura**: The best Okonomiyaki can be found at *Okonomimura* beside the Parco mall, with many individual stalls serving various versions on an open hibachi grill right in front of you (as is typical for all Okonomiyaki). For a truly local dish, try the *Kaki Okonomiyaki*.

Nightlife

The Nagarekawa *(Naga-lay-kawa)* district, a stones' throw from Heiwa-Odori, is one of the top 10 nightlife areas in Japan. The area is host to thousands of nighttime drinking and dining establishments. The entertainment district is somewhat co-mingled with the red-light district and, as such, you may not be allowed into all establishments that you decide to try as you explore. That said, the area surrounding the Parco mall, just West of Nagarekawa, remains somewhat lively into the early hours of the morning, without the red-light aspect.

- Foreigner/ Japanese Mix: Molly Malone's Irish Pub, MAC Bar
- Nightclub: Barcos, Club Leopard

Attractions

- **Peace Memorial Museum:** If you're visiting Hiroshima, the *Peace Memorial Museum* and adjacent *Peace Memorial Park* and *Atomic Bomb Dome* are must see. The Museum itself displays many artifacts and exhibits detailing the story of the bombing, recovery and the efforts by groups advocating for world peace and nuclear proliferation.

  Immediately outside the Museum lies the *Peace Memorial Park*. The Peace Park is a somber and lovely park highly deserving of a walk after a visit to the museum. Walk directly out of the museum, past the Eternal Flame for Peace display (dedicated to the victims and burns 365 days/ year) and through the park. It was this location that was the target of the bombing. Walk through the park and within 10 minutes you will see the *Atomic Bomb Dome* across the river. Known in Japanese as "Genbaku Domu," this was the only building left standing after the bombing, due to the explosion occurring directly above it. A memorial ceremony is held here every year on August 6.

- **Miyajima Island and Itsukushima Shrine:**

Just 20 minutes train and 10-minute ferry ride South of Hiroshima lies Miyajima Island, home to the Itsukushima Shrine, a UNESCO site and one of the most famous sites in Japan, recognizable by the giant orange Torii Gate seemingly floating in the ocean. The island is home to ancient shrines, temples, friendly deer, beautiful forest and even a trail of hundreds of Buddha statues. You can hike to the top of the mountain (plan for at least 2 hours up) or take a cable car for beautiful views of the Inland Sea and surrounding islands. The crowds are pretty intense during the day, but to really get the full experience, stay overnight at a Ryokan. I highly recommend a day trip, at least, if you're in Hiroshima. To get there, take the local train from Hiroshima Station South towards Iwakuni and exit at the Miyajima-guchi stop. Follow the crowds East towards the ferry to take the 10-minute ferry across the Inland Sea. Enjoy the views of the many oyster farms and mountains along the way.

- **Hiroshima Castle:** Near the city center, easily accessible by taxi.

- **Mazda Museum:** Tours of the Mazda factory are given daily.

Fukuoka

Situated on the West coast of the southern island of Kyushu (1 of the main 4), Fukuoka is a port city with fabulous islands and beaches, great shopping districts, amazing food, lively nightlife and some of the most laid back and friendly people in the country (if Japan had a California, it would be Fukuoka). Easily accessible by the Shinkansen line, Fukuoka International Airport and even a ferry line from Korea, Fukuoka is the southern gateway to Japan and the hot spring haven of Kyushu. Japan's 7th largest city, one of my top 3 favorites and an especially great place to visit during the summer due to the many festivals and beaches.

Getting Around

The airport and the main train hub of Hakata are about 15 minutes apart by car and easily connected by bus as well. Your main methods of transport will be the train, bus or taxi and the accepted IC card in Kyushu is the Sugoka (JR Rail lines) and Hayakaken (Fukuoka subway) cards.

Like all cities in Japan, Fukuoka has various neighborhoods each with its own identity. Unlike other cities; however, you can easily settle in any of the areas I will mention here, and not have to travel too far for a well-rounded great time.

- **Tenjin (*Tin-jean*)**: Popular as a shopping destination, Tenjin is also a thriving entertainment district. The area surrounding the Tenjin Station is packed with department stores, restaurants, and nightlife. Not far from the train hub at Hakata, this is where most visitors and locals congregate for a good time.

- **Hakata:** Numerous department stores and hotels can be found near the main hub of Hakata.

- **Canal City:** The area in between Hakata and Tenjin is known for the giant mall, adjacent to the Grand Hyatt hotel.

- **Nakasu:** The river island in between Tenjin and Canal City. Known for its wild nightlife.

Where to Stay

The majority of accommodations are found in Tenjin and Hakata. A few hotels can also be found on the beach, and there are some camping options as well.

- Luxury: Grand Hyatt (Canal City), Hilton Fukuoka Sea Hawk (Momochi Beach), Royal Park (Hakata), KKR (Hakata), Katsuma Beach Resort

- Mid-range: APA Hakata Ekimae, Hyatt Regency, Plaza Hotel Tenjin

- Budget: Green Rich Hakata, Hotel Sunroute

- Love Hotel: Nakasu is the love hotel capital of Kyushu

- Hostel: Fukuoka Backpackers Hostel

- Airbnb has abundant availability in Fukuoka.

- Camping: Nakanoshima Island, accessible by ferry from Meinohama Port, is an island in the bay where camping is allowed on the beach. Bungalows and supplies can be purchased on-site during the summer.

What to Eat

One of the best food cities in Japan, Fukuoka is most famous for its Ramen, fresh seafood and spicy cod roe 'Mentaiko."

- **Yatai** (street side food stalls): Hakata style Tonkatsu Ramen is famous throughout Japan and is best enjoyed in the many street side stalls (Yatai) along the streets in Hakata and Tenjin at night. Slide in and just order "Ramen" and maybe a beer while you eat alongside a couple of hungry salarymen for a real cultural experience. Don't be shy.

- **Fukuoka Kaisen Sakaba:** The most famous seafood restaurant in Hakata.

- **Ganso Hakata Mentaiju** (*men-ta-ee-ju*): Specializes in Mentaiko dishes.

- **Big Banana:** This beach bar near the Fukuoka Tower at Momochi Seaside Park is complete with charcoal grills at your table and sand at your feet. A must if in Fukuoka during the summer.

Nightlife

The Tenjin area is the center of Fukuoka nightlife, sprinkled with tons of restaurants and bars. There are also some options in Hakata, while Nakasu has many bars, along with a high concentration of nightclubs, cabarets and hostess clubs. Each is worth a visit and neither one is a bad time. As Fukuoka has historically gotten less foreign visitors than Tokyo or Osaka, you'll notice that it seems more open and friendlier than some areas of Tokyo, especially at night when people are out to have a good time.

- Bar/ Pub: Morris Black Sheep (Tenjin), International Bar, Coyote Ugly
- Nightclub: Happy Cock, Sam and Dave, Club X, Club Cat

Attractions

- **Momochi Seaside Park**: Many beach parties and events in the summer. Don't forget to stop by Big Banana for a real Japanese beach bar experience.

- **Fukuoka Tower**: Adjacent to the beach, worth a trip up to see the sights from the top.

- **Nakanoshima Island**: Great getaway on a nice day, and you can stay overnight as well.

- **Maizuru Park**: Contains Fukuoka Castle.

- **Museums**: Food and Culture Museum, Asian Art Museum, Fukuoka City Museum

- **Festivals**: During the summer, Fukuoka has many festivals. The largest is the Hakata Gion Yamakasa Festival which occurs in July.

- **Kyushu Grand Sumo Tournament**: Held in November each year.

Sapporo

Located on the Northern island of Hokkaido, Sapporo is Japan's 5th largest city and home to the famous beer brewery and the annual Sapporo Snow Festival which draws thousands of visitors. The city was expanded during the Meiji Restoration and designed in the same layout as many Western cities, which adds to its slightly international feel. The island of Hokkaido itself could be considered the Alaska of Japan, with snow, skiing, abundant fishing and wildlife (yes, there are brown bears, salmon, and crab), and generally cold (during winter) and mountainous terrain. Its summers are mild and non-humid, which even alone gives it a very different feel than mainland Japan.

Getting Around

Daily flights from Tokyo Narita and Haneda airports are available via many different airlines, as well as other major cities in Japan. You'll arrive at the New Chitose Airport, about 30 minutes from Sapporo by JR train. Alternatively, you could take a bus for the same amount of time. If venturing out into other areas of Hokkaido (it's a beautiful island), you may be connecting at Okadake Airport, and you'll need to get there via the local trains or a direct bus available from New Chitose.

Once in Sapporo, transportation via local train and taxi is the norm, as is the case in most other cities. JR Sapporo Station is the main train hub, and you'll be able to link to all other cities and stations in the region from here. Of note (and similar to Hiroshima), trolleys are present in some parts of Hokkaido where the subways do not run, mostly some Western parts of the city.

Where to Stay

In Sapporo, there are really only two areas I would recommend staying in: Odori Park or Susukino.

- **Odori Park**: Close to Sapporo Station, Odori Park is where the Snow Festival is held, an elongated park 12 blocks long that also hosts many festivals during the summer.

- **Susukino**: The lively entertainment area of Sapporo, similar to Shibuya or Kabukicho in Tokyo. Walking distance from Odori Park.

What to Eat

Best known for its seafood and Miso Ramen, Sapporo is a great culinary destination year-round.

- **Sushi no Yamada:** Famous sushi in Susukino serving fresh fish from all the coasts of Hokkaido.

- **Yozora no Jingisukan** (Genghis Khan): Popular style of Yakiniku in Hokkaido which is supposedly named after the shape of the grill, similar to Genghis Kahn's army's helmets. Mongolian BBQ with onions and beef.

- **Nishitondendori Soup Curry Honpo:** Restaurant serving the famous "Soup Curry" of Hokkaido.

- **Sapporo Beer Garden:** A famous beer garden located in Genghis Kahn Hall, serving the best food from Hokkaido and cold Sapporo beer.

- **Ramen Kyowakoku:** Outside of Hakata, Hokkaido Ramen may be the 2nd most famous Ramen style in Japan. Must try to miso Ramen while in Hokkaido.

Nightlife

The nightlife district in Sapporo is Susukino. By the time you've reached Sapporo, you'll more than likely have visited Tokyo. Susukino is very similar to Shinjuku in Tokyo. After a night out, make sure to have some famous late-night Ramen in Ramen Alley.

- Bar/ Pub: Brian Brew

- Lounge: Gossip

- Cabaret: Looop

- Nightclub: Vanity, Alife, Pit, Riviera, Sound Lab Mole

Attractions

- **Sapporo Snow Festival:** The most famous event in Hokkaido and destination for many from both Japan and all over the world. Held every February in Odori Park.

- **Tokeidai:** Famous clock tower

- **Hokkaido Shrine:** Famous shrine

- **Winter Sports:** Hokkaido is a world-class destination for winter sports.

  Out of scope for this book, please visit Tsunagu Japan for more on that.

Okinawa

The Hawaii of Japan. The tropical Okinawa, in the southern Ryukyu Islands, is actually closer to Taiwan than mainland Japan, and is starkly different than any other area of Japan, both in climate and culture. As Okinawa was not annexed by Japan until the 1800s, Okinawans truly view themselves as "Okinawan," similar to Hawaiians in that they are Japanese citizens, but their culture is 100% Okinawan. With the capital city of Naha, Okinawa is famous across Asia for its beautiful beaches, US influence (most US bases in Japan are located in Okinawa) unique foods, karate, the oldest living citizens on earth and even a sake made from a poisonous snake called "Habu Sake." Japanese and other Asians alike flock to Okinawa year-round for the beaches, diving and culture. Despite the dark history of Okinawa as the site of the bloodiest fighting in the Pacific during WWII, Okinawa today is a tropical paradise full of wonderful people.

Getting Around

The only way into Okinawa for most is the Naha International Airport. Direct flights from Tokyo, Osaka, and Fukuoka are available via ANA, Japan Airlines and Peach Airlines (I recommend Peach for the cost). Once in Naha, you'll need to either board the Monorail, which only extends just north of Naha to Shuri, or find a taxi outside the arrivals to get to your accommodation if in Naha. Logistics in Okinawa are not nearly as easy as mainland Japan, as a public train system does not serve most of the island, and service in Naha is limited to one line.

If you are staying outside of Naha (there are no beaches in Naha) I recommend renting a car for your stay. This is one scenario in Japan that it makes sense to rent a car, as the beaches are well outside Naha, and it is not financially feasible to take a taxi this frequently. You will need an international driver permit (available via AAA in the US), and remember, drive on the left side of the road.

Where to Stay

Where to stay in Okinawa is going to be highly driven by your choice of activities you'd like to do while there. The Northern end of the main island is quite secluded and not a popular stop for tourism, while the beaches along the West coast and islands off to the west of Naha have some of the most scenic beaches you can find on the planet. With that said, getting around is an issue, and I recommend you rest your head in the area you're exploring. For that reason, I will break this up a bit differently for Okinawa and won't go into great detail for each one.

- **Naha:** The capital city located on the southern tip, Naha has many interesting historical sites, cultural sightseeing, museums and contains the international shopping and food street "Kokusai Dori." Worth a stay for a day or two, but not close to beaches or watersports.

- **West Coast** (Chatan, Ginowan, Sunabe, Yomitan, Ishikawa, Onna): Plentiful in beaches, hotels, and nightlife. Many large beach resorts are located along the West coast where it's not even necessary to leave the hotel grounds (though that would be no fun). This area also contains most of the US bases on the island, and even an area called Mihama American Village, which has lots of Japanese-style American food (go and you'll see what I mean), shopping and entertainment. I would recommend staying near here if you want to be in the middle of the island, but the traffic is horrendous.

- **Kerama Islands:** Islands just to the West of the main island, accessible by ferry. Contains smaller hotels and very nice beaches and diving. Overnight is recommended but day trips are possible, I recommend the Crystal Blue Persuasion charter for day trips and diving.

- **Miyako-Jima and Ishigaki**: Islands a bit further Southwest off the main island, accessible by plane, but even more secluded and beautiful. Go here if you want a true idyllic beach experience.

What to Eat

Okinawan food is quite different than Japanese food. Though you can find plenty of Japanese (and American) food here, Okinawan food is a class all its' own, and is somewhat foreign to even most Japanese travelers. Below are a few noted recommendations that can be found anywhere:

97

- **Goya Chanpuru**: Scrambled egg dish with bitter melon. Sounds nasty, but worth a try and I am told it's quite healthy.

- **Umi Budo** (sea grapes): Found in many Okinawan dishes, and incredibly healthy. In fact, said to be one reason Okinawans are the longest living people on the earth.

- **Rafute:** Simmered fatty pork similar to what you find in a Chinese pork bun. This is my personal favorite. It is scrumptious indeed.

- **Taco Rice:** A local creation owing its birth the culture clash that occurred in Okinawa during the immediate post-WWII years and now a staple. Sushi rice covered with taco meat, lettuce, avocado, tomatoes, cheese, and hot sauce. Must try and said to be a great hangover cure.

- **Habu Sake:** I will admit, not a food, but a sake made from a fermented Habu snake, a poisonous pit viper native to Okinawa. Said to produce some strange effects but considered safe. The locals will love you if you show the courage to drink it.

Nightlife

As with Okinawa as a whole, the nightlife is going to depend on your location on the island. In general, due to the high numbers of US servicemembers, most nightlife areas will have a different demographic than other places in Japan, and at times may feel more like the US.

- **Naha:** Naha has its fair share of restaurants, bars, and nightclubs. Start out at Kokusai Dori.

- **West Coast** (Chatan, Ginowan, Sunabe, Yomitan, Ishikawa, Onna): Each of these areas has its own host of things to do after dark, with the highest concentration of bars around Gate 2 street near Kadena air base. Note that many places have a high concentration of US servicemembers.

Note: If driving a rental car, keep a note of the fact that the blood alcohol limit in Japan is 0.03%. This means that even after 1 drink you could easily get a DUI. Use a local service called "Daiko" (die-ko) which will drive your car (with you in it) to your accommodations after a night out (don't worry, they won't stay with you). Ask the establishment to call them, it's what all the locals do.

Attractions

- **Churaumi Aquarium**: The 2nd largest aquarium in the world and home to captive whale sharks.

- **Shuri Castle:** Ancient head of the Ryukyu Kingdom.

- **World War 2 Sites:** Japanese Navy tunnels, Sugar Loaf Hill, Peace Memorial Park, USS Emmons

- **Kokusai Dori** (International Street): Lots of food, bars, and shopping. #1 daytime tourist area in Naha.

- **Murasaki Mura:** Traditional culture and entertainment park.

- **Maida Point**: Viewpoint for famous coral cliffs.

Acknowledgments

I would like to thank those dear friends I made while living in Japan who enabled me to see things I would have never seen, experience things I would have never experienced, and grow to love a culture that I would never have truly known. Also, to those friends I experienced this beautiful culture with.

Domo arigato gozaimashita,

Dave

Made in the USA
Middletown, DE
26 June 2021